MW00785015

Encore:

A Collection of Poetry

Zaneta Varnado Johns

Encore

Published by Prolific Pulse Press LLC
September 2023, Raleigh, North Carolina USA

Copyright© 2023 by Zaneta Varnado Johns

All right reserved under International and Pan American Conventions. No part of this book may be reproduced in any manner without written permission from the publisher, except in the case of brief quotations embodied in critical articles and reviews.

Library of Congress Control Number: 2023915855

ISBN Paperback **978-1-962374-00-2**

ISBN eBook **978-1-962374-01-9**

Cover Design: Kelli R. Jackson
Interior Graphics: Kelli R. Jackson
Interior Design: Lisa Tomey-Zonneveld, Prolific Pulse Press LLC

Dedication

Words can travel thousands of miles.
May my words create mutual understanding and love.
May they be as beautiful as gems,
As lovely as flowers.

~Thich Nhat Hanh~

I planned to publish one book—one and done. I am the author of three poetry collections, three collaborative books, and the *What Matters Journal*. Tell me what God won't do! For every relative, friend, poet, and organizational leader who pushed, prodded, nudged, and encouraged me to share beautiful, lovely expressions: this one's for you. I titled this book to acknowledge your continuous and much appreciated applause. I heard it. I responded. This is your encore—from my heart to yours.

Perpetual gratitude to my ancestors.
To my future generations: This is for you too!

Contents

Previously Published

Poetry Collections
*Poetic Forecast: Reflections on Life's Promises, Storms,
and Triumphs*
After the Rainbow: Golden Poems

What Matters Journal

Collaborations
*Voices of the 21st Century: Resilient Women Who Rise and
Make a Difference*
*Voices of the 21st Century: Conscious Caring Women Who
Make a Difference*
Voices of the 21st Century: Women Transforming the World

Co-Editor
Social Justice Inks
Dear Heart

Featured in numerous international anthologies
and literary publications

Website: ZanExpressions.com

Encore

Acknowledgements

It is my distinct honor to have poems selected as worthy of award recognition and inclusion in distinguished literary publications. Some features may reflect earlier versions of the poems herein. Thank you to all of the dedicated editors who present our expressions to the world.

Poetry: The Best of 2022, Poets of the World, "Secrets Inside the Moon Shadows"
October Mania, "A Kiss for Paris"
Armchair Poetry Anthology: The Flowers and Butterflies Edition, "Valley Love"
The Literary Parrot: Series 4, "Blessed Life"
A Safe and Brave Space Volume 2, "My Home, My Refuge"
Rainbows and Daydreams, "Daydreaming: We Have Enough"
Beautiful: In the Eye of the Beholder, "The Beauty Within"
Harbinger Asylum Anthology, "Seasons"
Chaucerberries Anthology, "My Heart Has Checked-in Full"
Fine Lines Journal, Summer 2023, "I Know What Love Looks Like"
Gifts Anthology, "Aloha Anniversary Gifts"
Scars Anthology, "First Prize Scar"
Fine Lines Journal, Spring 2023, "Her Empty Garage"
Movement: Our Bodies in Motion, "Move on, Ms. Simone"
Jewels in the Queen's Crown, "Move on, Ms. Simone"
Fine Lines Journal, Summer 2023, "Fifty-two Sunrises"
Contemporary African Women Writers, India, "Her Words Speak for Me"
Dear Heart Anthology, "Mother Tell Me a Story—Yours"

Encore

Atunis Poetry, Belgium, "Loving Hands, A Fusion of Love"
Zooanthology, "The Owl, My Raptor of Love"
Humanity Magazine, March 2023, Russia, "Hello Blue"
Social Justice Inks, "Now You Know"
We Rise by Lifting Others, India, "Poetic Call to Action"
A Spark of Hope-Volume 2, India, "My Promise as You Heal"
LOVE Anthology, Bengali, "Innocent Love"
Bards Against Hunger 10 Year Anthology, "Hunger, A Global Tragedy"
Love is a Divine Fragrance Anthology, "Stop Harassing"
The Talk, "My Talk with Jerron-1997"
Humanity Magazine, Russia, March 2023, "We Train for This"
The Literary Parrot: Series 3, "Why I Write"
Inked with Passion, "Twisting Toward Totality"
Fine Lines Journal, Autumn 2023, "We Are Fine"
Voices of the 21st Century: Women Transforming the World, "Soaring Intently"
Cultural Vision Anthology, "Elementary Pleasures"
Nobody Told Me It Would Be This Hard, "Empty Nest"
NLHF 6-Lines Poetry 3rd Place Award, "Quantity and Quality"
Passion of Poetry *Poet of the Week* April 9, 2023, "Empty Nest"
Passion of Poetry Grand Champion April 15, 2023, "Why I Write"
Passion of Poetry *Poet of the Week* May 21, 2023, "Honoring My Mother"

Deal with yourself as an individual, worthy of respect and make
everyone else deal with you the same way.
~Nikki Giovanni

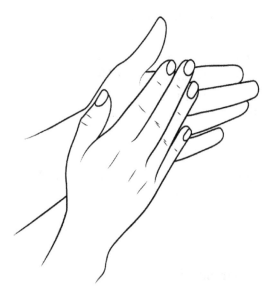

Foreword

Chyrel J. Jackson

Zaneta Varnado Johns' *Encore*, her third poetry compilation, is an encapsulation of the spirit of Aloha. It is that precise spirit that runs deep within the soul and writing of this commanding international poet. It is the through line and common theme that unifies the poems within *Encore*.

Love of all things would be the second most powerful thread throughout *Encore*'s pristine messaging: Love of self, family, friends, community, nature, travel, and life itself are all universal themes explored within this imperial and timeless collection of poems.

It is an honor and privilege to bear witness to one of our generation's most prolific voices of contemporary/modern poetry.

Encore rises to every measure presented. The poems are majestic, thoughtful, and magnetic. The final rendering is a delicate, soft, and well written solid inspiring life mosaic.

From New Orleans, Hawaii, Colorado, and Greece, *Encore* delivers a great prism of unmatched emotion and skillfully penned verse.

Appropriately numerous signature poems from Zan's previously published features make a second appearance in *Encore*: "Joy in Her Swing," "Aloha Anniversary Gifts," and "Soaring Intently," among others.

Encore

It is the intention of this collection of poems to more than
greet its readers with the spirit of Aloha, but to also welcome
them into the emotionally charged universe of Zan Johns. I'm
here for each poem herein hanging on her every sublimely
written word.

Encore is the perfect follow-up to *Poetic Forecast* and
After the Rainbow: Golden Poems.

Zan once stated, "I believe that every word shared is an
opportunity to love." All Zan's poetry books, especially
Encore, empower each of us to do just that. It is my hope that
these heart sculpted poems will be revisited and often shared
time and time again.

Whispers and Romance

Encore

Romantic Intention

Four sparkly eyes
fixed on the setting sun
We are one—
a romantic spectacle
of hopeful intents

We move as one
hand in hand
We inhale as one
Every breath rife
with twilight air

Blissful moments of
romantic intention
sealed by
golden promises

Our tender embrace
bouquet of gardenia
and tranquility
Aloha!

Encore

Hold Me Close

When you hold me
Nothing can harm me
The world is brighter
I am safe

When you hold me
My thoughts are clearer
My spirit rejoices
I am free

When you hold me
I sleep sounder
My dreams are deeper
I am renewed

When you hold me
The clouds hold promise
The earth is treasured
I am serene

When you hold me
The birds sing shriller
Flowers bloom fuller
I am entranced

When you hold me
My winter's warmer
My summer's cooler
I am bold

Encore

When you hold me
My faith is stronger
Heaven is nearer
I am redeemed

Encore

Secrets Inside the Moon Shadows

If moon shadows had voices
what secrets would they tell
Whose stories would reveal
their plunge under the full moon's spell

How many passionate words were spoken
Love songs sang, slow dances danced
How many promises were broken
when lives beyond the shadows advanced

The night's luminance is just enough
for secret meetings in the meadows
As darkness stirs intense passion
it sparks secrets inside the moon shadows

When the moon casts its twilight
through branches beneath the trees
Distorted images suddenly emerge
as illusions of love in the breeze

Plans conceived with starlit eyes
Lovers' hands held and intertwined
Eager luscious lips—tenderly kissed
under the influence of the shadowy bliss

Many a heart unwittingly seduced
beneath the moonbeam's silky sway
Some fragile hearts—sadly smashed
as jilted lovers ran astray

Encore

Emotive fragments were deserted—
a scattered puzzle to later seek
Teardrops left on the summer grass
shattered souls unable to speak

Just think of all the deep secrets
inside the full moon's shadows!

Encore

A Kiss for Paris

Someday I'll arrive in Paris
surrounded by lovers from right to left
I'll carry an empty suitcase
'cause as a shopper, I am deft

I can't wait to sip the wines
speak as though I'm French
I'll sit among worldly travelers
in parks on my favorite bench

When I touch and kiss the Eiffel Tower
my red lipstick will be proof
that I love this romantic city
that I conquered its allure with oomph

This dream I've had forever
I know it will come true
Paris has lived within my heart
since the carefree days of my youth

Encore

Our Dance

Hello, my love, you had me at "Hello"
The spark of your soul set my soul aglow
Our love's slow burn triggered my desire
The passion between us lit my heart's fire

This journey we're on has borne luscious fruit
Our harmonious dreams, a steady pursuit
Now we dance a new literary waltz
A two-step of sorts, poetically taught

This time around I lead the dance
Please never let go of my inking hand
Let's enthrall viewers with our graceful moves
Let's charm the world with verses that soothe

Together we are a charming pair
No room between us, plenty love to spare
When your heart pulsates, I feel its beat
When your mind wanders, my muse repeats

We became one in spirit and soul
A quarter-century later, our lives are whole
Thank you for choosing to dance with me
God assures me that our best is yet to be.

Encore

Chillin'

Steady raindrops—inspiration
I feel especially rich today
I watched a poetry podcast
Life is grand, I must say

Red wine is my beverage
My snack is cashew nuts
God blesses me lavishly
No ifs, ands, or buts

My husband loves me dearly
His adoration I do treasure
My love for him is evermore
in more ways than I can measure

Encore

When Love Lingers

Carry me to our realm of bliss—
to our evergreen forest
where we forever kiss

When love lingers
our songs never end
Our dance begins and begins again
I am smitten… my mind spins
Tenderly, our hearts blend

When love lingers
lustful smiles appear
Fanciful dreams sneak in
My sleep flows into hot air balloons
We drift into the far beyond—swooned

When love lingers
the air is fresh
Every breath is ours
Every breeze is ours
Goosebumps blanket my flesh

When love lingers
oceans become baths
Waves wash away my fears
The sun bakes my skin
No more tears, heaven is here

Encore

When love lingers
our past is now
A perfect collision
to secure our love
forever

Encore

Night Waltz

You came to see about me
Throughout the night we danced
Pure passion and romance

No pandemic, no darkness
Just light and music
You and me
I was surprised
totally mesmerized
to be encircled once more
in your loving embrace

My heart raced
We smiled and laughed
Our spirits pranced
We waltzed
In synch, our limbs and feet
As one—our happy heartbeats

Like old times
together and free
Free to love
Free to hold each other
until the sweet dream ended

Encore

On a Whim

I was seduced
by the wind
Alone, I listened closely
for your sweet tone

Led by the crescendo
of my dancing heart
I yearned for that whisper
It rocked my vulnerable soul

Your scent is a holiday
You take my breath away
Ecstasy engulfs my airway
Oh how I wish you could stay

On a whim, you knew
that moment would be
like the last spoon
of ice cream—
leaving me longing
for more

Encore

Quiet Thoughts

Could the paper stand the heat
in my smoke-filled kitchen
if I cooked what
I was too young to crave
I'm not that brave
to venture down the path of
the long ago past

When that car showed up
I showed out
I'd rush inside
Heart outran me every time—
a homerun for him

I watched him round those bases
Young passion took me places
Tank tops, strappy sandals, short shorts—
Hot pants, Daisy Dukes
Call 'em what you want
Just hit a home run for me

Call me when you get home
I waited—yearning
to hear that special voice
I stayed in your corner
because in my adolescent heart
every corner belonged to you

Encore

Valley Love

A blooming love in the valley
Two hearts frozen in time
On slippery boulders they frolicked
Creek rushing
Love's intensity followed
It would remain this way
Forever intertwined

Life happened
Their bodies singly yielded
Decades passed
Though held by other arms
It is that playful time
That remains with them
Nearly fifty years later

Life marches on
Waters still rush
Whispers still echo
Songs still sing
Precious moments intact
Love still lingers
That space in the valley
Belongs to them

Encore

Our Kiss

my heart dances long after our kiss
no other soul makes me feel like this
impassioned tango on faraway sand
four synchronized footprints
ever forming—never the same
daring steps lighter
hearts aflame

radiant sun in a perfect world
clarity, hope, charity
bells ring
magic beneath my wings
utterly smitten by your charm
surrender, sound the alarm
in a fixed state of longing
my heart dances long after our kiss

Encore

Water Play

Misty waters
waterfowl, seagulls
water play—
duck-duck-goose
Inside my car
I duck too
Love is contagious

Beware the fishermen on your left
He's mine
no matter the chill
rod and reel
crab as bait
he wades in the water
he patiently waits

He reels-in another empty hook
yet he's still content
It's like a good book
can't tear him away
not today
water play

Peace times two
I can watch him for hours
That's our true love's power!

Encore

Changed

Unfailing trade winds
render a satiating breeze
Eastwardly across the ocean
sweet air sets us at ease

We slow our pace
turn face to face
Everyday pressures plunge
our souls fuse with grace

When the sun kisses the ocean
passion flares as darkness rings
Nightfall presents too many options
to do what makes our hearts sing

So we exult and sing
lyrics of our new love found
When our bodies tenderly embrace
we are eternally bound

Essences

Encore

Blessed Life

I live. I breathe. I celebrate.
Freely. Gloriously. Gratefully.
I feel compassionately
I love unconditionally
I move intentionally
I forgive graciously
I rejoice constantly
I listen attentively
I see delightfully
I share willingly
Unapologetically, I am
the person that God
called me to be

When I stand with my sisters
I am whole
I am authentic
My confidence soars
In their presence I am safe
We balance each other
We support each other
We crave the chance
to celebrate each other
Together with my sisters
We live and flourish

Encore

From earth to sky
I savor all that I see
I am but a mustard seed
in this vast universe—
significantly insignificant
I look up and ponder
What is beyond the trees
I peer through the light
Infinity is what I see
That is but a small portion
of what God has for me

Encore

He Did That for Me

When God created the universe
He did that for me
When He laid down the Ten Commandments
He did that for me
When He gave us freedom of choice
He did that for me

When God chose Mary to carry His son
He did that for me
When He sent Jesus down to Earth
He did that for me
When Jesus walked and lived among men
He did that for me
When he forgave those who betrayed Him
He did that for me

When our loving Savior died upon that cross
He did that for me
Three days later when He arose
He did that for me

Encore

My Home, My Refuge

Home is an open door
arms wide-open
Familiar voices
approving eyes, fresh air
No airs, no judgement—just bare truth

Bare feet up, guards down—
absolute ease
A circle of everything I love
A love of everything that encircles me

Home is good food
The sound of music—or silence
Room to dance—or just to be

Home is warmth on the coldest days
Refreshing coolness to defeat the heat
A soft landing when I'm spent
Pillows of comfort for my muse
No facade—only love behind these closed doors

Home is precious memories
A breeding place to create more
A house of prayers and hope for others
My balance is here—I am centered
I have no fear—I trust entirely
My home—my refuge—fosters my well-being

Encore

Willows at Boston Commons

String music cheers the park
Weeping willows reign
Human rainbows stroll singly
some in pairs
Little girl finds a perfect branch
for her upside down
adventurous self

Shades of yellow leaves
announce autumn
Books and blankets adorn the park
Ducks and geese parade gallantly
across the pond
Dogs walk their owners
Inviting benches hold contented souls
Playful toddlers teach parents to trust
Cheerful chatter resounds

On this glorious October day
the sun dances behind the clouds
At every chance light filters through
the wondrous willows
Green branches sway with subtle gusts
With my other half beside me
I sway too
Filled with pleasure
my spirit dances with the sun
sways with the willows
at Boston Commons

Encore

Daydreaming: We Have Enough

I daydream all day, I daydream at night
I hold my pillow snug and tight
My dreams are filled with sunshine and rain
A blissful life without any pain

Abundance is the baseline in my world of dreams
We all have enough—life is serene

Enough love to comfort our spirits
Enough validation to be our true selves
Enough food to nourish our bodies
Enough respect to embrace all people
Enough confidence to celebrate our friends
Enough humility to be free of boasting
Enough trust to erase all fear
Enough empathy to understand others
Enough compassion to wipe out loneliness
Enough courage to try something new
Enough laughter to breed happiness and joy
Enough forgiveness to heal any sorrow
Enough challenge to expand our learning
Enough imagination to create new works
Enough presence to appreciate nature
Enough grace to embrace all humanity
Enough reverence to live in peace

Encore

The Early Bird

Dawn announced the early bird
Throughout the day its voice I heard
It roams from shrubs to banyan trees
It flutters above with songs of glee

Birds serenade in verse and prose
Sweet sounds atop plumeria or rose
Chirps resound all over the land
on grass… over waters... deep in sand

Its tweets surpass my comprehension
loudly bellowed to get my attention
I wish the croons I could understand
I listen closely wherever it lands

I can't help but envy its carefree life
Birds have no worries—no human strife
These creatures exude freedom and grace
They help us endure the trials we face

The rooster's crow I ignore
I dismiss the sounds of traffic
Delightful is the nearby song
The early bird makes me happy!

Encore

Wise Summons

The wise owl beckons
even when it sleeps
Omnipresent I sense its soul
Its great wisdom is mine to reap

The vocal owl croons at dusk
I'm awakened by late night hoots
No matter where I might be…
meekly heartened, I uproot

The fleeting owl spreads its wings
Its majesty is most secure
Praise songs, my aroused heart sings
Mesmerized I am, for sure

My soul communes with the souls of others
whenever a wise owl appears
My attention it grabs without a choice
Our mystical bond is forever clear

Encore

Virginia Musings 2022

light morning fog
dense trees
humidity
summer heat
filtered sun
sprawling branches
wild turkeys
baby doe
owl on high
nature prevails

on winding roads to everywhere
traffic flow not flowing
present company present
across the drawbridge
over the Potomac
we creep
patience required

steep narrow shoulder
eye-level tree line
too many trucks
I smile inside
happy to ride
with my brother
on our way
to Ohio

Encore

By and By

I am—
Led by love
Anchored by awe
Pierced by peace
Seduced by serenity
Guided by gratitude
Encouraged by empathy
Comforted by compassion
Mentored by morality
Focused by fierceness
Bound by benevolence
Driven by desire
Cast by courage
Governed by generosity
Heartened by humility
Built by bravery
Renewed by resilience
Transformed by tranquility
Nudged by nobility
Coerced by charity
Wowed by wisdom
Gifted by goodwill
Lifted by loyalty
Pursued by patience
Tempted by truth
Delighted by determination
Protected by prayer
Altered by aloha

Encore

Table for Two

Still I set a table for two
I sit beside an empty chair
The joys we shared between us
warm my soul as if you're there

I now see the plans you had for us
with every seed you planted
The fruits of your deliberate love
I will never take for granted

Through the eyes of others and mine
your vision has become quite clear
I'm surrounded by nature's bounty
These blessings return every year

I gladly accept and honor these gifts
by sharing with those I love
I hope you're pleasantly satisfied
as you watch me from above

Encore

Catfish on a Red Plate

Living good is
catfish on a red plate
sizzling hot
bones or not
Hot sauce handy
Appetite required
Table optional
Gather

Chilled beverage—
carbonated
Rhythm and blues—
down-home preferred
TV off or on
Good company
So much history
So much love

Time almost stands still
Ready to face
whatever comes
This is home
This is ritual
This is rich
Living good is
catfish on a red plate

Encore

The Beauty Within

I am smiling on the inside
because it is beautiful here.
Beautiful because I woke up this morning
Beautiful because my family has expanded
Beautiful because I am authentic and healthy
Beautiful because I am loved
Beautiful because I generously spread love
Beautiful because praying gives me goosebumps
Beautiful because forgiveness brings healing
Beautiful because I share my abundance
Beautiful because I cheered a sulking soul
Beautiful because I set stones for others
Beautiful because I reach for your hand
Beautiful because I found my passion
Beautiful because I make a difference
Beautiful because memories transport me to beauty
Beautiful because I respect mother earth
Beautiful because I cannot step on an ant.

When you see my smile, you see the beauty within.

Encore

Seasons

After
the season
of summer ends
I mourn its presence
I dread winter's approach
I prepare for Fall
I dislike cold
I retreat
inside

Still
I'm happy
I await Spring
The budding of trees
The birds build their nests
The rain brings promise
of fragrant flowers
Colorful honey
bees

June
is back
I am thrilled
This cycle of life
reminds me to be glad
for God brings forth
whatever we need
We're blessed
Amen!

Encore

Access Granted

My Father in heaven is always free
When I need a friend
He's there for me
When the world is cruel
He comforts me
My cup cannot hold
all He has for me

His precious blood covers me
A divine shield protects me
I have the fortitude to succeed
My blessings are perpetual
Access to His power is granted
provided it serves His purpose

Encore

Replenished

Mountains and sky
Green into blue—
or the other way around
Outdoor pleasures abound

Rolling hills of
sage and brush
Splendor in the skies
slows my mind's rush

Flora whisks me toward open space—
an alluring and healing place
Tantalizing paths to travel
Burdens slowly unravel

Animal sounds fulfill
Aromatic terrain heals
Everyday worries left behind
Inner peace I find

Fertile ground feeds
I follow cosmic leads
My mind and soul
spiritually pleased

On inviting rugged trails
I discover a gentle ease
I accept and receive
all that nature offers me

Encore

My senses are ecstatic
Blessings inherited long ago
Overcome with endless gratitude
I am replenished in this meadow

Encore

Life As a Breeze

If I were the wind
I could go where I please
I could be calm
I could be fierce
I could be soft
I could be swift
I could roar

I would sway unpredictably—
from gentle to strong
My gusts would command
your undivided attention
I would be nameless

If I had no gender
or color—like the wind
might I be more welcome
might I be safe
might others not fear me
might I be privileged

Might my life
as a breeze
be splendid

Encore

My Heart Has Checked-in Full

Patiently, I stood by—
trusting that God had more
instore for me
Along came you,
and my heart checked-in full.

Full of joy and laughter
Full of happily ever after
Full of wonder and surprises
Full of sunsets and sunrises
Full of travel and so much fun
Full of battles already won
Full of God's amazing grace
Full of hope for the human race
Full of balm for untimely sorrows
Full of promise of bright tomorrows
Full of compassion generously hurled
Full of peace throughout the world
Full of chances to make a difference
Full of gentleness and reverence
Full of families realigned
Full of a future redefined
Full of cups that overflow
Full of love that grows and glows

Encore

My Walk Along the Ocean

Merrily I walk along the ocean
Majesty is mine
Fiery sun blankets my back
Pristine waters at my right
I follow my shadow—
my keen island guide
on this bright sultry day

I absorb the ethereal landscape
path sprawling with magic
I warily travel along the lava—
extrusive rocks formed ages ago
I heed variations of
rugged black texture
Razor-sharp formations
command caution and praise

I am seduced by harsh grey stones
covered with lichen
Aromatic winds pervade my body
My spirit blooms—
one step closer to heavenly bliss
Tropic birds summon me
I look up
Aloha consumes me
I exult with utmost gratitude

Encore

Hawaii Fishermen

The ocean breeze cools and teases
Fishermen watch anchored poles
Fresh bait and lure await
Serene patience grows

Fish swim in sapphire waters
as waves rush
as fishermen wait
They appear in their own sweet time
as rolling sprays bellow
Surf crashes against the rocks

A faraway silhouette—
just close enough to see—
perches atop the ancient rock
His exotic tattooed legs dangle
below white shorts
A torso flaunts a burnt orange tee
A camouflage hat tops it all
Colorful is my favorite fisherman

He leans forward
Did he catch something—
or is his line hooked
I wonder…
who's the real catch
on this warm windy
tropical day

Encore

Fall Upon Us

Fall arrived too quickly
But God, I didn't do x, y, and z
Dear, none of that really matters
What counts is what you did for me

I saw you help your dying friend
When she was fearful you had her back
You made time for vital things
I will never forget that fact

Whenever a loved one needed you
you offered the best of yourself
You knew that in the end
your generous soul is what is left

Even when you were tired—
when body aches slowed you down
You never once complained, my dear
You deserve a golden crown

Your kindness makes the world better
You love deeply while you're here
Moreover, you inspire my people
Your voice will linger for years

41

Encore

Empty Nest

The nest was never intended
as a permanent place to stay
Our birds we must surrender
as we watch them fly away

We nurture and we mold them
while they are in the nest
When it's their time to venture out
they've already passed the test

It's not the birds I fret about
They fly away without fear
We parents may need comforting
Our next move is not always clear

Do we leave their rooms unaltered
Should we call them everyday
Do we trust that they are ready
to handle any trial they face

When my birds left their nest
Grateful tears I shed with glee
I changed their rooms to office space
So they could no longer live with me

I love my children dearly
These birds are flying high
Their wings will not betray them
On my love and wisdom they rely

Encore

I Know What Love Looks Like
Inspired by John Palmer

Love doesn't always travel through hugs
or bedtime stories, or "toesie" rubs
Love may be silent—not a word expressed
No "*I love you*s," no verbal caress

Love might appear as "absent while present"
Love bought with money is quite unpleasant
Love disguised as discipline confuses the child
Whose thickened skin may take a while

Love in the form of hard work is pure
Love's unattended children come to be unsure
Love may not applaud your every success
Love's absence at key events can cause distress

Love may not say "Yes" when you crave it most
Love can seem distant though your hearts are yoked
Love may not share keys to the family's car
Love prays for you nearby and from afar

My friends, I know what love looks like
It's not always what you expect
Love's intentions are mostly admirable
but can be illusive with great effect

Encore

Nothing can dim the light which shines from within.
~Maya Angelou

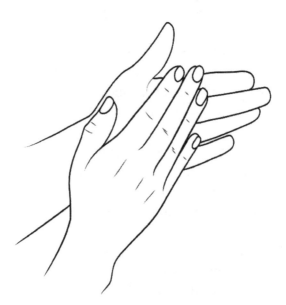

In Awe

Encore

Honoring My Mother

Dear Mother, as you watch us from above
savor the many fruits of your forever love
I know you are proud and divinely blessed
Your children and grands are doing our best

Do you tell the angels all that you see
as you smile down on us continuously
Our lives are filled with love so deep
yet at times your absence makes me weep

Tears sometimes rush like the river's flow
I'm comforted by your essence wherever I go
I summon your sweet voice whenever I choose
Your precious memory I will never lose

You emboldened a merit I cannot explain
This knowing is as certain as sunshine and rain
With wind under my wings, I rise with grace
I will honor you throughout my earthly race

Encore

My Grands

I adore the patter of ten little feet
all over my house
They bolt up the stairs
and down again—on repeat
Five grands playing hide-and-seek
Hushed laughter as I try to sleep

My heart could not be fuller
Neither could their bellies
Early breakfast with fruit
Innocent fun, their main pursuit
Low and high pitch tones
boys and girls
toys and curls

Fresh snowfall awaits
What will they create
They'll soon bolt outdoors
after pretending to do chores
Happy tears fall
I love it all

Topaz twins
Garnet boy
Sapphire girl
Citrine boy
A ring for every finger
Precious memories linger

Encore

Four little feet moved to Seattle
Six now living in Arkansas
What's a grandmother to do—
My bags are packed!

Encore

Elementary Pleasures

The simple pleasures in our
segregated classrooms were parties—
tuna on crackers
grab bags of goodies
names pulled
modest gifts traded—
our festive time before the holiday break

We had secondhand books and
first class teachers—
Mr. Davis, Mrs. Porter,
Mrs. PJ Harris, to name a few
Best friends for life
Ties bound on short walks
up and down Mooney Avenue
Lured daily by our segregated park
with elementary pleasures
I loved the swings

I'd stroll past *The Stand*—
Mrs. Theresa's sweet shop
Oh how we craved
the two-for-a-penny cookies
red hot fireballs and pickles
Now and Later candy and gum
Delightful elementary treasures

Encore

My hometown—still my happy place
My parents no longer with us
Still love and comfort await
in the home of Ms. Laura Knighten—
devoted educator no longer in the classroom
At ninety-three she still teaches
at every opportunity—
Known for special treats and
constant elementary pleasures
Known as the embodiment of earned esteem

Encore

Our Brother, Our Gift
For Anthony, at Sixty-five

Separated by mystery, miles, and decades
Bound by blood, bayou, and blues
Long ago, a crucial seed was planted
A nagging question—unasked
We led full lives amid a void
Muddled and undisclosed until now.

Wonder and love triumphed
Science made a way
for the collision of our DNA
You found us though we were never lost
Neither were you
Only time ... was lost.
Did our youthful paths cross, I wonder
Innocence ruled but our spirits must have known
How else can we love you so deeply?

Our brother, our gift
You are patience personified
A classy and charming man
Attentive and caring son
Adoring father, doting grandfather
Enthusiast of wine and cigars
Lover of rain, trees, and all things good
I can't wait to learn more
Promise you'll play your drums for me.

Your musings travel in waves of baritone
past our grandmother's bright smile
Our daddy's essence returns

51

Encore

His stature commands our attention
Delightful reels of our childhood flash before us
What we have is now
We are the stars—past and present
Our future awaits.
God chose the time
We chose the reception—
Welcome, our brother, our gift!

Encore

First Prize Scar

Boldly she reveals her tummy's scar
This distinct mark carried her thus far
Marvelous that she is not ashamed
of the wound required to heal her pain

That scar portrays a warrior's strength
Her will to live—tested at great lengths
This teen now thrives in whatever she does
Her light reveals God's grace and love

Most people shield their scars from view
Her confident spirit is daring and true
Fearless she is—wholly unfazed
Awarded first prize for winning life's race

Encore

Aloha Anniversary Gifts

My soul shouts *aloha* and *hallelujah*
because you love me out loud
Aloha gifts of silver and koa—
perfect for our special day
when God joined us together
twenty and five years ago

Your gifts could not be
more thoughtful, more perfect
unrivaled actually…
because you know my soul

You know my heart's happy beat
because you trigger it
You know my elated smile's silhouette
because you drew its lines
You know my hopes for our tomorrows
because together we imagined them

Our yearnings are infinite
Our most coveted desires live
in the arch of that rainbow—
delightfully placed before us
on this tropical February morning—
another divine gift of aloha!

Encore

When Time Stood Still

Frozen in darkness
Lush with pain
Death has a way
of having its way

The clock stops
I retreat inward—
my symbolic return
to the place
where it all began

My shattered heart was hollow
My numb body had nowhere to go
I nestled inside the safest place I know—
the imaginary womb

I can hardly rest
I am distressed
because you're not here

My world lacks
the most precious love
I've ever known—
my mother's

Encore

Her Empty Garage

Once cluttered to capacity
Love permeated this space
once upon a time
Then life happened
Wall-to-wall pain crept in
and stayed…

Her garage—now empty
A beautiful site
filled again to capacity
with love—
top to bottom
side to side

Love replaced unspeakable pain
of loss—
a daughter gone to soon
a granddaughter left behind
a terminal illness
Then time stood still…

Love showed up
in friends and family
who gathered
to clear the chaos
Their steps ordered
Their souls determined

Encore

Her beautiful past resurfaced
when stashed treasures were shared
as blessings to others
Her love will travel
to homes near and far
as her soul rejoices—hallelujah
She blessed so many
without having to lift a finger

The empty garage reflects
the love she gave—plus
the love given back to her

Encore

Storm, When We Helped Our Friend
For Roxie

Like shadowing storm clouds
darkness encircles our circle
yet the sun illuminates our way
We follow the divine light
We show up because
God trusts us to do His will

God knows our hearts because
He shaped them
He filled us with kindness
and waited…
and watched…
He knew we would help
our friend-in-need
It could be no other way

God named us *Selfless*
Unconditional was our guide
Judgmental was not present
Compassion led the way
He ordered our steps
We followed His commands
Above all, *Love* ruled the day

Encore

Joy in Her Swing

Filled with awe and wonder
the young girl peers above
Toward her heavenly angels
who rest in peace and love

A bright new beginning
in her cozy new home
Warmly welcomed and showered
by loved ones she has known

This blessed little girl
has seen far too much
In her short five years
many lives she has touched

Her mother transitioned to heaven
Her grandmother left in charge
For the next three trying years
grief was a constant sparge

God then summoned her grandmother
to His heavenly home to rest
His plans for this precious one
arose in a friendship manifest

By car Azaria traveled
to Florida with her loving auntie
Open arms and hearts were waiting
at her perfect destiny

Encore

She is adored beyond measure
with little Diamond in tow
Her beloved pet Chihuahua
goes wherever she goes

Now joyful in her swing
Her life is obviously grand
God's light shines through her bright eyes
just exactly as He planned

Encore

At a Standstill
  For Steven Lester Carr

I received the news
on the bus
in the mountains
no reception
unable to respond
at a standstill
so I write

Utter sadness
rocked my soul
disturbed my peace
inspired my creativity

You touched so many lives
including mine
Your generous praise
propelled me
to write even more
At a standstill

I write to honor you
Suddenly, your legacy
shouts… shines… sparkles
You changed the world
So many short stories
So many poems
So many gifts
for generations to come

Encore

Who knew that "The Gift"
Would be such a poignant gift—
certainly not your last gift
At a standstill—I'm writing
Thank you, Steve, for your encouragement
Thank you for the sublime works of amazing literature
Our world is better because you lived!

Encore

Move On, Ms. Simone

Nina Simone would gallantly glide across the stage
forging a seismic shift in perception of what was beautiful.
She opened her mouth and belted out our anthem—
"Young, Gifted and Black."
These moving words lifted the ego of a people—my people
She transformed a gloomy stigma into immense pride.

She sashayed toward her piano with purposeful intent
Her dance revealed a story, a message of sorts
The subtle sway of her head and neck
portrayed undeniable sophistication
Her poise, an understatement
Her song, a powerful statement!

Her hands wed the keys—a match made in heaven
When she left the piano, her stride was fierce
Her manner and movement could pierce
Her melodies had a movement of their own
The Civil Rights Movement anthem tops her musical
throne
Now in heaven, Ms. Simone walks the streets of gold
May her graceful movements forever be told.
Her grace was sufficient... Move on, Ms. Simone!

Encore

Fifty-two Sunrises

It was on your terms, My Love
Within the sanctuary of our home
Fifty-two days, our last lap as we once knew
with your dignity preserved
We did it our way—together
Just us, enveloped in our perfect space
We faced the foreseeable
with courage
We learned so much
We shared intently… attentively
lovingly… spiritually
Just us—in our own way

Your comfort reigned
Your presence triumphed
Precious memories made
Desires expressed
Plans paved, promises cemented

As the appointed time neared
Meticulously you offered your best self
A little sorbet for your pleasure
I amplified your single rose ask
by twenty and four
You deserved that and so much more

Encore

In the end, a lovely rose for you
As I delicately held your hand and head
twenty-three buds of rose petals
gently surrounded you—
deservedly in every way
Anticipation heightened
A divine blessing offered

My beautiful Love, carefully wrapped
in the folds of select cloth
As you left, a lone red petal
jumped from the cloth
in a determined circle toward me—breathtaking
Thank you, My Love, for your parting gift
You, my forever gift, live deep within my heart

Encore

Heaven's *Tornado*

Our interlocked arms are fewer
but our friendship circle is intact
We encase the souls of our beloved *Tornadoes*
who never completely disperse
Tornado trails of memories live on
as an EF-5 level love that cannot die

Fun stories and laughter sustain us—
church and music
dance and mischief
secrets and successes
friends and families—
All are treasured within our unique
HHS 1975 Tornado circle

Though another voice is silenced
Her heart still speaks to us
Her encouragement still guides us
Her fine example still awes us
She is loved for how she loved—
cherished for how she lived

Daughter of a local legend
Jane Caroline Moore Perry bridged
the roles of wife, mother, grandmother
sister, aunt, colleague, and friend
She leaves an indelible mark
on all who knew her
The sun still shines on us
Our purple hearts are full

Encore

When God called, Jane expected it
A woman of God does not worry
when her time comes
Rather, she consoles others
Her grace and gratefulness prevailed
In response to God's call
our friend grasped His unchanging hand
and to all of us she said—
See you later

Encore

Her Words Speak for Me

When Phillis Wheatley penned religious and moral
expressions
She spoke for me
When she defended her publications—triumphantly and
unprecedented
She spoke for me
When she fearlessly unleashed great vulnerability
She spoke for me

When Maya Angelou exclaimed the joy in her feet
and the grace of her style
She spoke for me
When she shared gifts from her ancestors
She spoke for me
When she asked us to know and do better
She spoke for me

When Nikki Giovanni claimed that pyramid
She spoke for me
When she adoringly honored her mother
and encouraged our daughters to dream
She spoke for me
When she demands a citizen's right and responsibility to
vote
She speaks for me

When Tracy K. Smith ponders the intended purpose of our
souls
She speaks for me
When she imagined the emotions of Einstein's mother
She spoke for me

Encore

When she proclaims the painful truth of our nation's
declaration
She speaks for me

When Emi Mahmoud slams with love and conviction
She speaks for me
When she moves through sorrow using the power of her
words
She speaks for me
When she lauds her mama's bold resilience
She speaks for me

When Amanda Gorman climbs that hill
She speaks for me
When she declares victory over speech hurdles
She speaks for me
When she exhibits excellence and distinction
She speaks for me

When Elizabeth Ogunmodede climbs that ladder to the top
She speaks for me
When she shares sound lessons from her Nigerian
grandmother
She speaks for me
When she expresses her love for literature
She speaks for me

Encore

May future generations speak for me
May they walk our well-worn path
Their way is clear—
illuminated by our legendary footprints
May brilliance travel in giant leaps
over the tongues of
not-yet-born African American girls
as they speak for me

I expect lessons learned—a less arduous journey
I expect our voices to resonate far into the future
I expect reflections of my complexion
I expect excellence and inspiration
whenever she speaks for me

Encore

Mother, Tell Me a Story—Yours

If only you could tell me a story
I would pour us a cup of tea
I would settle into a comfy chair
I would give you all of me

I would listen to every single word
Your life's story should be heard
Tell me all the juicy good stuff
Tell me about when times were rough

Tell me the wildest of your thrills
I want to hear all about your fears
Talk about playing on those red dirt hills
during your Mississippi childhood years

Please share the details of falling in love
Were there combatants you had to shove
Were there suitors you unintentionally hurt
What songs and scents ignited your flirt

I want your secrets, lessons, and heart's desires
Share any regrets that oft transpired
I know you have a lot to say
Speak slowly, Mother, I'm here to stay.

Encore

Loving Hands, a Fusion of Love
    For Renee

"Will you be there," your yearning heart asks
"Will you be with me when our precious Lord
takes my hand…
When He calls me to His promised land
will you be there?"
My spirit silently answers
"My heart will always be with you, Mother
I will tenderly hold your hand
as long as God allows—
just as you assuredly held my hand
all my life…"

I entered this world a helpless babe
You held me and loved me
You gave me everything I needed
You added everything I wanted
You held my tiny hand
before I knew how to hold yours back
I soon learned to firmly grasp
the hand that would nurture and soothe me—
the hand that embodied confidence
Yours is the hand that loved out loud
The hand that shouted *hallelujah* in praise
The hand that fed our family
with food from your soul—soul food
The hand that weakened with time
as life induced new trials

Encore

Strength traveled serenely
from your hand to mine
I humbly receive your power and grace
As I cling to your still-warm hand
I receive the best of you
We are inherently bound—
a fusion of endless love
a love adequate to sustain me
This precious moment will present itself
within my heart
for the remainder of my natural life
plus forever in my grateful soul

Encore

To Love You
    For Kathy

I can only imagine what your backpack held
With your Eurail Pass, two worlds you would meld
Adventurous wonder nudged you on your way
Kindness was your superpower then and today
I wonder if you see what we all see
How you live your life phenomenally
I admire your light and overall ease
You go about your day determined to please

A teacher you are and will always be
The knowledge you share flows constantly
It is joyous to witness your conversations in Greek
I'm enthralled by the attractions you continually seek

Your home is an extension of your generous heart
I saw your selfless spirit from the very start
It is my pleasure to know you… we are intertwined
Our forever friendship gets better like wine

Do you realize, Kathy, how special you are
Your warm-hearted nature reaches near and far
Do you know that your smile travels through your voice
The endless joy you extend gives others no choice

But to love you…

Encore

The Owl, My Raptor of Love

You visit me whenever you please
Your essence leaves my mind at ease
Ever since you first quietly appeared
Perched on my deck, I had no fear

Welcomed, your visit, I knew why you came
You shared that heaven was now your domain
Your voice softly soothes me, at dusk or late night
I adore your wingspan when I watch you take flight

I've observed you atop my neighbor's roof
You watched me closely, not seeming aloof
We are spiritually connected, I am assured
When I hear your wild voice, my heart is lured

Legend says bad things follow your appearance
But my mother's promise gives my soul deliverance
Sometimes you say things I'm not ready to hear
If a loved one passes, you will reappear

Many say you are wise
I'm not in the least surprised
You know more than most people
You shield us from evil

Your hoots serenade me for extended times
Whatever you impart is oft divine
Nocturnal and day raptor, I am in awe
You are highly revered under nature's law

Encore

Umoja Toast

Here's to the ones no longer here
Here's to the ones who follow
From my heart's core
I pour libations of adoration

In remembrance and reverence
Here's to my great great ancestors
who toiled without reward
whose freedom was deprived
even before they were born

In remembrance and awe
Here's to my grandparents
who were proud and strong
who loved fiercely
who sacrificed for my parents

In remembrance and appreciation
Here's to my parents
who loved me out loud
who laid a foundation of trust
who taught me hard work
who instilled my self-worth

With infinite gratitude and expectation
Here's to my descendants
In the spirit of Umoja
One by one, I honor you

Short and Sweet

Encore

Quantity and Quality

How many tomorrows and pages will I fill
How many wounded hearts may I help heal

How many sleeps before I never again wake
How many sunsets and prayers will I partake

How much love will I have known
How many souls will bless my own

Encore

Talking with My Heart

I talked with my heart the other day
It took time to say what I had to say
I disagreed with what it said to do
Bravely I stressed my point of view

When temptations clash with my heart
uneasiness prevails from the start
No doubt my heart is the ultimate boss
My contesting ideas I eventually toss

Encore

Misty Shield

At times we need a misty shield
over this troubled land
Sun still shines above the clouds
Light filters through—
glimpse of heaven

Beneath the blanket of fog
we pray for peace
we invite stillness
Across peaks and pastures
when the sun returns
watch for the rainbow—
God's promise

Throughout valleys and vistas
voices ring atop the trees
Joyful sounds among the shadows
celebrate the fleeting wonders
beyond the clouds

Encore

Inside Looking Out

Inside looking out
world in turmoil
Amid pain and fear
love holds the key
I remain hopeful

I see a world of possibilities
I see courage
I see untapped compassion
I see hope
I see willing warriors
who endeavor
to make a difference

March with us
Change the world

Encore

Ask for Goodness

When sky meets earth
formed as a rainbow
expect goodness—
expect promises fulfilled

Delight in the breathtaking spectrum
of God's amazing grace
Misty waters hold the answers
to life's most unwieldly asks
Ask for forgiveness
Ask for gentleness
Ask to end hunger
Ask to stop violence
Ask to revitalize the earth
Ask to unite our world
Ask to heal all humanity
Ask to shine your light
Ask to increase your territory

Encore

Beyond

I wonder what's beyond
Beyond the rocks—
jagged and settled
atop the shoreline

Beyond the shimmering sand
Beyond the waves
Beyond the deepest blues of pristine waters
Beyond the fishes below
Beyond the trees—dense and green
Beyond the clouds over the horizon
Beyond the stars—the celestial sky

I believe with all my heart
There is a world of promise—
a world of possibilities
Beyond…

Encore

Wishful Thinking

Hurting hearts healed
Mental illness mended
Physical pain purged
Lonely souls lifted
Furious actions forgiven
Homeless families housed
Hungry mouths fed
Forgotten memories recovered
Peaceful presence restored
Generational wishes granted

Encore

Obedience

He shaped our hearts
Filled them with kindness

He waited…
He watched…

We performed
as He knew we would
It could be no other way

Encore

Pineapple Hill

In the not-too-far distance
on Pineapple Hill
rests a glorious landscape—
Carved-out carpets of
uniform green grass

Intended for golfers…
none in sight

Lavish luxury
abandoned development
left to become
Maui's most accidental bike path
in sight!

Encore

Baby Fish

Fisherman hooks a baby
He returns it to the ocean
So shines his benevolence

Baby fish returns to water
Given a second chance
it swims far away

Inevitably the fish is hooked once more
Will the baby meet kindness again
or become someone's dinner

Encore

Hello Blue

Well hello blue!
All week long
I've been waiting for you…
I knew you were up there
beyond the clouds
in the open sky air

I've been down here
wet from the rain
The cold chilly wind
held me constrained

I settled indoors where it's cozy and warm
My peaceful retreat away from the storms

I listened to music, poetry I did write
I read blissfully, sometimes 'til midnight

Now that I see you peek through the clouds
I'm heading outdoors to live out loud!

Encore

Curtain Call

When the curtain opens to tomorrow
what will the stage reveal
Will the actors remember their parts
Will special effects help me heal

The last show was too painful
So many props I despised
Characters were out of character
I abhorred their disguise

I recalled all our lines
today when I arose
I penned this to let you know
the staged drama has been closed

Encore

Boundaries

I said "No" when *Anxiety* arrived
When *Overwhelmed* showed up
escorted by *Unannounced*

I said "No" when *Fun* was absent
When *Crisis* took the wheel
without a license

I said "No" when *Appointments*
surprised my calendar
When *Demands* grew
paired with *Excitement*

I said "No" when *Family*
needed my attention
When *Obligation* triumphed
Stressed set some boundaries
and I said, "No."

Encore

On My Way to Heaven

On my way to heaven
I take my precious time
I wouldn't dare rush
my journey on earth
Mindfulness feeds my soul

On my way to heaven
I listen to God's every word
I claim every promise
I accept every trial
I heed every instruction

On my way to heaven
I hold onto God's unchanging hand
My other hand clutches my loved ones
We create precious memories
to soothe them
long after I am gone

Encore

Glorious bouquet and storms of applause are the
trimmings which every artist naturally enjoys.
~Golda Meir

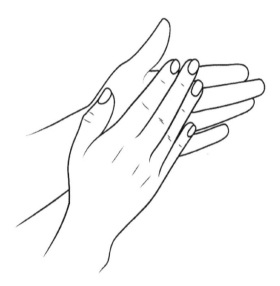

Rants and Spiels

Encore

Now You Know
   Honoring Congressman John Lewis

Had they known he would be a noble statesman,
would they have hosed the protesters on Selma's Bloody
Sunday?
Had they known he was there to spark "good trouble,"
would they have let their horses overrun the crowd?

Had they known he would lead this nation's Peace Corps,
would they have cruelly beaten him with Billy clubs?
Had they known he would compose great books and
legislation,
would they have intentionally fractured his skull?

Had they known he would sit across from US Presidents,
would they have defended Jim Crow and corruption?
Had they known he would secure voting rights for all,
would they have tear gassed everyone within reach?

Had they known he would rise in American history,
would they have brutally knocked him to the ground?
Had they known he'd be called "The Conscience of
Congress,"
would they have called him all those terrible names?

Had they known he'd receive the Presidential Medal of
Freedom,
would they have forcefully and repeatedly locked him up?
Had they known he'd lie in state as an honored official,
would they have deterred his crossing of that bridge?

Encore

There is at least one "John Lewis" in every peaceful
protest.
No excuses—now you know!

Encore

Poetic Call to Action

Let's place a poem on the path
of the next plotting killer
May our expressions be the answer
May our voices be the healer

When someone aims to hurt
our sisters or our brothers
let's travel within their minds
Toxic thoughts we'll uncover

If we tenderly hold their hands
surely their troubled hearts will follow
We must fill them up with love
in the places where they're hollow

If we caress their cold-hearted bodies
I believe their souls would heal
Please answer my call for action
Noble poets, let's all get real

I trust your indelible pens
I humbly ask you to trust mine
Our mission is beyond crucial
Together we must heal humankind

Encore

It Has to Stop

Moments of silence add up
as silent leaders covet power
Too many hours wasted
Too many families devastated yet again
Stop the violence!

Again our nation mourns
without adequate scorn
of society's violent thorns
We failed our children
failed to protect
failed to act
failed to lead
failed to model what we expect from them

What do they think of us, I wonder
Do they feel abandoned—at school
Do they trust us to shelter them
Is violence their norm
We sorely need reform—
reform our hearts
reform our intentions
reform our response

My tolerance wanes as the next killer plots
to torture the have-nots
Where is the innocence
None of this makes sense
Let's draw the line on crime
Summon the keepers of my brothers
Please someone protect my sisters

Encore

Handguns are more present in schools
than kindness and prayers
Rifles attend churches and theatres
as if they're supposed to be there
Automatic pencils are surpassed
by firearms—automatic

Children kneel to hide rather than to pray
Dreadful to see children
running away
from school—
away from learning
Flags at half-staff are red flags
Empathy we lack when
mental health is debated
after-the-fact!

Target practice on humans must end
Practice love instead, dear friends
End the debate over guns and semantics
Helpless beings are frantic
We must restore sanity
for the survival of humanity!

Encore

My Promise as You Heal

If you'll let me into your world
I promise I'll be gentle
If you'll allow me to hold your hand
I will walk with you step by painful step

If you'll allow me to see the darkness
I will illuminate it with utmost care
If you'll allow me to share your burden
your load will become less heavy

Trust me to hold that gun
Trust me to discard those pills
Trust me to remove all harmful weapons
Trust me to be present as you abandon that bridge

When you trust and surrender to my promise
your life will go on
I promise to stay with you throughout
and to love you as you heal

Encore

Innocent Love

Tender hearts are born to love
Innocent reliance on others
for coexistence and survival
is inevitably rewarded
or crushed

Innocent love is not jaded
Innocent love is nonjudgmental
Innocent love sees only good
Innocent love expects only good

Innocent love quickly forgives
Innocent love is kind and giving
Innocent love lends our best selves
Our earnest innocence
loves unconditionally

Encore

Hunger, a Global Tragedy

Hunger happens when humanity fails
Our most basic human need—unmet
Swollen bellies, empty stomachs
Desperate souls—abandoned
Eyes wide open, no hope in sight
Clean hearts, dire circumstances
People are starving!

The tragic contrast is an abomination
Tunnel vision void of compassion
Deep pockets, too-full bellies
Greedy souls, willful waste
Blind society, access denied
Blissful hearts, luxuries abound
People are satiated!

It is not too late to help
the helpless
the hopeless
the homeless
the hungry

Malnutrition is a human condition
Silent cries—weak, shaky, and lightheaded
A global cacophony of growling stomachs—
inhumane
Stop, look, and listen
People are dying!
It is almost too late
for far too many!

Encore

What Does Your Mirror Say?

Social accountability begins in the mirror.
Honest reflection is required.
What does your mirror say?
Would it praise your actions, reactions, or inactions?
Would it judge you as you judged the needy?
Would it ask why you ignored another's cry?
Would it praise your demand for equality for all?
Would it scold your reluctance to help others?

It confuses the mirror when you look away
or when you smile as tears well up.
Sincere reflection is priceless.
Does the mirror hear your heart's rapid beat?
Does the mirror sense any contempt for diversity?
Does the mirror frown because it sees no compassion?
Does the mirror question your silence?

When the mirror examines your intention,
will it see indifference or
your devotion to social justice?
The next time you look in the mirror
I hope you like what you see.

Encore

Not Eclipsed

I won't be eclipsed
My shaded shade
is here to stay
I'm utterly content because
God made me this way
Hate has no place
Respect my skin and face
We are all the same within
Hatred is a sin!

God is displeased
with this growing disease
Animals, trees, and other species
come in all colors—
none better than the other
It is absurd to hate *black* or *brown*
Unjust to grant *white* the ruling crown

It's foolish to cherish the aspen's trunk
Irrational to treat evergreens as junk
Prejudice makes no sense
Our decline is too intense
Please reset your hearts and minds
Halt the demise of humankind!

Encore

Deep Pain

With sandpaper you wipe
my weeping eyes

Tears created by the buckets
of venom you spewed

A heart so cold
I can see the Northern Lights

Your once loving eyes—
now daggers of ill intent

Your hug—a weighted blanket
a deceptive cover

Your altered spirit rivals
the grimmest villain

A dead silence reminiscent
of the day before creation

If we pull the trigger on this facade
I'm sure it would hurt much less

Encore

What Men Do

What men do
was the elephant
in too many houses
My upbringing
told me
that it was okay—cool
Almost a birthright
for men to cheat

A man is just being a man
He's doing *what men do…*
I didn't question
whether this was
a southern thing…
a Louisiana thing…
I didn't ask,
"Do all men do
what men do?"
Black men
White men
Married men
In-a-relationship men…

Encore

What men do
told eager young boys
and naïve young girls
that men were privileged
That although men loved their families
it was their right to stray
Afterall, a hard-working man
deserved time away…

We grew up!

Encore

Compassion

Pain travels as quickly as love—
perhaps faster
I am not okay until you're okay
For humanity, I kneel and pray

I ask for healing
I ask for comfort
I ask for no one to be alone
Leave no one behind

Compassion is the conduit
Extend the best of self
Eradicate greed
Lend a hand… or two

I give what I can—
the best of myself
plus so much more
I yield to the divine design
of our universe

Encore

Stop Harassing

How can she concentrate
with a tortured mind
internally bruised
externally battered

You didn't have to touch her to hurt her
Your words and jokes
Your lewdness and posture
are more than enough
They are—
not welcome
not funny
not acceptable!

Hostile imposition—intentional or not
If she is uncomfortable
by what you said
If she feels threatened
by what you did…
Take heed!

She is emotionally compromised
Safety is not solely yours
Her space is not yours at all

When you rob her of peace
You stunt her progression
Your laughter costs you nothing
Yet it costs her everything!

Encore

Selective ignorance is not a free pass
Wake up and learn
Learn and listen
Listen to her cues—
silenced and spoken
Stop harassing, period!

Encore

Resilience

Negativity cannot stall us
Misguided doubt certainly fuels us
Losses may slow us down
but beware when we get up

Our voices won't be silenced
We embrace our inner child
Tenacity is our weapon
Inequity gets us riled

We nourish and follow our passion
We willingly do the work
We flourish when we listen
though the truth may sometimes hurt

In the end we are rewarded
with triumph to match our faith
We take nothing in life for granted
Watch us surely soar with grace

Encore

Inner Thoughts

You wouldn't want
to know my thoughts
Down deep within
are ugly sins
of my father's father
and his father too

In this world around us
no one protects us—
so it seems
So in my corner I sit
I search for me
I escape to a place where
all around me is good
from the inside out

World upside down
like my life
My smile turns down—
involuntary frown
You wouldn't want
to know my thoughts

Encore

My Talk with Jerron-1997

New house, new town, new hopes
Old stigma, old pains, old fears!

"Hey Ma, I'm going for a run," said Jerron
"No, not yet, let's talk," I cautioned
I thought of others who were taunted—
some even killed while going for a run…
"We just moved here. No one knows us.
The sun will soon set…
Not yet Son, not just yet!"

It was 1997—no cell phones—no protests—
Just a mother's knowing
"You are seventeen, a promising young man to me
To them, you are an imposing black figure—
a threat—someone to fear
They don't want you here!
To them, your life has little value
To me, prejudice is a serious matter!"

"Son, I see you, an honor student
A star athlete with a heart of gold
They see breaking news—headlines
with threatening black images in the stories told
I see my only son, my pride and my joy
They see someone unequal—insist on calling you, "Boy."
I see my collegebound student who excels in science and
math
They see a scary dark figure approaching them on the path
I see a fine young man whose body is his temple
They see someone to harm and call it accidental

Encore

I see a bright future, a future attorney in fact
They see nearly two-hundred pounds—
strong, dangerous, and Black."

"So, I can't say *yes* to your run just yet
I love our new home and life
but our new city, we have to vet.
You see, our dilemma is wrong and so unfair
You have only one life, no extra to spare

For you, society offers no benefit of the doubt—just doubt

For others, the privilege is two-fold, at least
For you, work twice as hard—like a beast
For others, 'Get out of the car' means *Let me help you*
For you, the approaching siren signals a risky pursuit."

"Remember a full tank, working lights,
and active signals are must
Don't speed, don't swerve, above all, don't trust!
Draw no attention to your car
A traffic stop might go too far
Should you ever be pulled over,
make no sudden moves
Hands up, follow orders, respond as the officer rules."

Encore

"I'm sorry I can't guarantee
that my advice will always work
Each time I think of it, my heart breaks and hurts
No mother should have to worry
about her child with the police

After all, don't we pay them
to be officers of the peace!"

Encore

What If

What if tomorrow never comes
Would you pursue joyful pleasures today
Would you spend your time with others
Would you covet shrinking time alone

Would you continuously say *I love you*
or would silence rule your day
Would you spend your time in gratitude
or would you seek worldly possessions

Would you notice the lovely flowers
or would you ignore nature's abundance
Would you reach for another's hand
or would keep yours to yourself

Would you explore celestial wonders
or would you cultivate the soil
Would you read and watch a movie
or would you recall lifelong pleasures

Would you listen to good music
or would you delight in fading silence
Would you breathe with reflective ease
or would you tensely wait for the end

What if...

Encore

We Train for This

We train for this,
the spokesman said
more than once—assuredly
I've actually heard it
more than I care to
after more mass shootings—
city after city…
state after state…
Mass shootings
throughout our country—
the United States!

As our first responders
train for this
Why don't the rest of us
train for kindness
train for reverent life
train for helping those
whose mental health
screams for help!

Train to act *before* hatred strikes
Train to restore hope
where hope is void
Train for selflessness
Train to gladly serve all people
Train for our planet's endurance
Train to restore humanity…
Let's start training now!

Keynotes

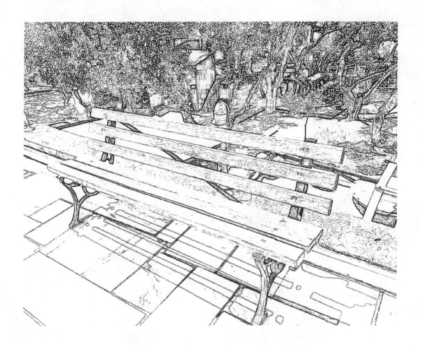

Encore

Why I Write

I watched Nikki Giovanni trip over her ego
I witnessed the phenomenal Maya Angelou rise
How could I not be totally mesmerized!

Countless strong women preceded me
surrounded me
nurtured me
I honor them as I nudge the next wave
of strong women to
write
          trip
                    rise.

My pen— my weapon—my best friend
Mouthpiece for my muse
It remembers what Nikki said
It remembers what Maya said
It remembers what my parents said
It shares my truth as it repeats what God says.

I write to spread love
I write to heal, help, and honor
I write to leave a footprint—my literary mark.

I want my great great great grandchildren
to know that I was here
I want them to know how and what I felt
I want them to speak their truth
I want them to know what matters.
This is why I write.

118

Encore

Which Story Will You Tell?

The blank canvas beckons
You hear a cacophony of young voices
Faraway—from ages ago—quiet too long
They scream, yell, wave, and stomp
Anything to win your attention
Anything to be selected…

Listen closely to their screams
Those little girls—today's prompts—
have stories to tell.
The hopscotching, roller-skating,
rope-jumping, hand-standing,
hula-hooping, jacks-playing,
sing-songing, monkey-barring,
Miss Mary-Macking little Zans…

The curious one who asks no questions,
silenced when told to speak when spoken to
The one with tissue in the toes
of her too-big, pointed-toe shoes
Or the one whose tight shoes were worn too long,
hoping a parent would notice
because she didn't want to ask

The one who squinted extra hard during her eye exam
because she longed to wear glasses like her mother
Or the one who stood on an empty glass,
not expecting it to break and cut her foot

Encore

The one enticed by Creole smells that permeate
the too-small kitchen
The girl who, with her siblings,
could no longer stand the aroma
of freshly jarred fig preserves—
who broke the seal of every jar
to taste just a little

The one who patiently waited for
the always-occupied sole bathroom
The one whose skinned knees didn't deter her
from kneeling in dirt or on blistering asphalt
to shoot marbles for keeps

The one who baked mud pies until
called inside at dusk
The one who played four-square
in the middle of the street—who scattered with others
as the car's horn beeped… and brakes screeched

The girl who savored the plump plum
secretly plucked from her cousin's tree
Or the one who fearlessly trudged through the woods
to pick blackberries, oblivious
to the snakes that slithered along her path

The girl who was regularly chased by stray dogs
in pursuit of more than friendly licks
or pats on the back
The one who coveted every role
in school and church programs

Encore

The carefree girl who pursued butterflies,
dragonflies and grasshoppers
The one who relentlessly sought four-leaf clovers
and refused to step on an ant
Whose story will you share first?

Encore

The Poet's Pillow

It's not your standard pillow talk
With inspiring words we talk our walk

On pillows we dream of a kinder world
Nocturnal ideals freely unfurl

Pillows give comfort while we sleep
Nightly notions are often deep

Pillow-talk musings—our divine calling
illuminate conditions we find appalling

Pillows shake as our minds construct
Routine sleep patterns our thoughts disrupt

While the world sleeps our brains awake
Ideas roar as expressive earthquakes

We rejoice because we're on a mission
Our lyrics enhance the human condition

Encore

We Are Fine

We are a grid of creative potential
not locked… not perfect
We are strong
Iron sharpens iron
We refine our lines
before, during, and after camp
Read between our lines
We are fine

Once broken
we gathered our pieces
one by painful one
The light shone through
Our spirits triumphed
We reassembled
with wisdom and vision
We sealed our pieces
with golden expressions
We are a work of art—
fine art

Induced by the blank canvas
we are curious
We go outside with nature
where endless potential awaits
We go inside ourselves
where the truth lives

Encore

the real stuff
good… bad… ugly
We fill the canvas
line after line
We are *Fine Lines*

Encore

Simple Creed

Prayer works when we faithfully believe
Believing is effective only when we act
Actions speak volumes when paired with giving
Give what you can—most of us have enough
Enough is enough… don't overlook the needy
Needless to say, covet sacred things
Things of substance must comprise justice
Justify efforts to mend what is broken
Break the cycle of poverty and loneliness
Lonely hearts lead to beliefs impractical
Practice only what you brazenly preach
Preach about what matters—love
Love everyone as you love yourself
Selfless service is simply honorable
Honor the hopeless…the helpless… the homeless
Homelessness invites and pervades all colors
Color your world with compassion and kindness
Kindhearted people make a difference
Differences are compelling with infinite beauty
Beautiful is our world when we support each other
Another's trials cast shadows on humanity
Humans are meant to live in harmony—
a simple creed!

Encore

Serenity

Serenity is—
where the cicadas serenade
where baby doe takes her first step
where wild turkeys trapse across the meadow
where a child's wonder fills her days
where possibilities are infinite
where life is carefree
where the landscape sings
where colorful kites fly
where trees clap to greet me
where rippling waters tickle tiny toes

My soul celebrates—
when my imagination begins and begins
when nature receives as it generously gives
when lovers frolic in the rain
when boat sails are lifted
when snowflakes slowly linger
when a last wish is granted
when perfectly painted sunsets appear
when the full moon rules the sky
when eternal promises are sealed

I wrote this expression
for reasons unknown…

Encore

Undo Hurt

She yearns to unsee deceitful acts
She wants to un-clap her hands
She will un-sing those songs of
adoration and praise
about her unfaithful lover

She must unplan her wedding—
uninvite two-hundred guests
She must take care of her unloved self
Allow God to do the rest

She feels unworthy and betrayed
unable to embrace faith, hope,
the unknown
Underneath her deepest pain, she fears
that she may not be able to cope

She uncovered their love's façade
unclogged her naïve ideals
To reclaim her true self
she unplugged that relationship
and unleashed sad thoughts
In time, she will unravel all hurt
and move on…

Encore

Joy Ride

Freedom behind the wheel
I tossed you out the window
kept driving
didn't look back…
Drop-top down
Open sky canopy
My passenger is the breeze

My enticing future
gets closer with every mile
The distance between myself
and my baggage—
between you and me—
grows farther… sweeter…
comfortably vast
You are my past

My load is light
I yearn adventure
The wide-open road
of daring lanes
twists and turns
arouse my inner thrill
Joyfully I ride
Sincerely
I wish you well

Encore

Twisting Toward Totality

Dare I go left or veer to the right
Do I look toward the sky or the ground
I'd rather go over instead of going under
I'd much rather smile than to frown

Should I stay in, or should I go out
Must I remain silent, or scream and shout
Shall I take a friend or travel alone
Inside my mind is where I'm most at home

Am I destined to win, or will I lose
Sometimes I question the path I must choose
At times I feel tangled from head to toe
When my insides are knotted, the ideas flow

I'm like the twisted tree in fertile soil
My passion requires courage, devotion, and toil
When challenged, I easily bend and turn
Thriving and inspiring are my main concerns

My perfect imperfect spirals are by design
These answers to life's woes are uniquely mine
This enigmatic stature secures my strength
It nourishes my imagination at notable length

I do not envy trees straight and tall
When crises approach, I'm not prone to fall
Foes dismiss me from their plan of attack
With loving expressions, I'm prepared to fight back

Encore

My wholeness exceeds what your eyes can see
I adapt to shifting demands brilliantly
Tightly clinging to my roots binds my spirit
Though all tied up, my gnarly knots have merit

I fearlessly yield to the higher power
Absorbing light and energy by the hour
I rejoice at my capacity to endure life's storms
I am strong and mighty, not at all deformed.

I'm like the twisted tree—twisting toward totality!

Encore

Soaring Intently

Together we soar, sister-to-sister
We stumble, we recover, we rise
Hand in hand, we are heartened
Arms locked, shoulders down
Chins up, voices unmuted
We take our time
Step by intentional step
We oversee our destiny—we take charge!

Minds opened…bodies healed
Relations mended…fears conquered
Outlooks brightened…selves loved
Goals achieved…careers changed
Finances tended…hope restored
Grief consoled…faith deepened
Courage expanded…wisdom gained.

We are butterflies in flight
We delight in our freedom—
freedom borne of trials and thrills
From our favored spaces around the globe
transformations flourish—
spontaneous and deliberate
We are authentic… unscrambled
Our puzzled pieces—properly placed
Wounds healed… internal fires ignited
We are whole and wholesome!

Encore

Watch us sparkle with eyes transfixed
on that beacon of goodwill ahead
There's no looking back—except to evolve
We know better... now watch us do better
Watch us ascend purposely
Watch us bolster our communities
Watch us uplift the children
Watch us love unconditionally
Watch us transform the world!

Encore

Greece

I see Greece in my rear-view mirror
magical land of abundance
vast beauty exceeds account
My perspective is forever changed
enriched frame of reference
I covet the view ahead—
a tempting lure

Venus smiled nightly upon us
from expansive starlit skies
Earth shows us how to live
Generous is land richly blessed
by light and water
Land tended by villagers in no rush
Wisdom shines in the intention
and attention

Fertile soil takes seed and proliferates
rewards without discrimination
From one seed, many uses
From one flower, many nourished

History holds true today
Folklore teaches all humanity
Christianity is one story
Greek mythology another
The brain is not new, just refined
The window to the world is open
It's up to us to explore and learn
To Greece, I must return

Encore

The Line of Great Poets
*Inspired by LaVan Robinson and Lisa Tomey-
Zonneveld*

When the pearly gates flung open
I loomed and boldly entered
God summoned me to follow
holding my hand amid the winter
I looked all around me
for the loved ones I had known
I was ready and obedient
when He gently called me home

I had no worries, fears, or doubts
that I was worthy of inclusion
I had lived an honorable life
My destiny was not an illusion
I had but one essential concern
as I walked through heaven's door
May I join the line of great poets
carefully chosen by God to soar

I did everything I could
to say what God asked me to say
My intention was to speak truth
and spread love everyday
When God called my name again
my anxious heart skipped a beat
He directed me to that line of choice
Now I can deservedly rest in peace

Encore

About the Author

Zaneta Varnado Johns, aka Zan Johns, is an award-winning, 4-time bestselling author of *Poetic Forecast* (2020), *After the Rainbow* (2022), and the *What Matters Journal* (2023). Johns is a contributing author in the Women Speakers Association's #1 international bestsellers *Voices of the 21st Century* (2021, 2022, 2023). Her poems are featured as the Dedication page in these collaborative books.

Johns co-edited *Social Justice Inks* (2022) and *Dear Heart* (2023) with publisher and poet Lisa Tomey-Zonneveld. She serves as an editor for the *Fine Lines Literary Journal* and administrator for the *Passion of Poetry*, a revered online platform for emerging and esteemed poets. She is a Pushcart Nominee in Poetry and a USA Contributor in the Russian Guinness World Record *Hyperpoem*. Her poems appear in nearly seventy anthologies and international literary publications. Believing that every word shared is an opportunity to love, Johns' writing offers hope as she stirs the reader's consciousness about life and living.

Johns is a retired human resources leader who spent her twenty-nine-year career at the University of Colorado. She was recognized in 2007 as one of the University of Colorado's Women Who Make a Difference. Johns resides in Westminster, Colorado, USA.

ZanExpressions.com

Personal Publications by Zaneta Varnado Johns

ZanExpressions.com

Gratitude

I know that God loves me because He surrounds me with an incredible circle of esteemed creatives and fans. I hear their loud continuous cheers even when I sleep. I wake up ready to please, ready to deliver what they ask. With gratitude, I open the curtain to introduce *Encore's* behind-the-scenes crew:

Publisher:
Lisa Tomey-Zonneveld, publisher extraordinaire and the founder and manager of Prolific Pulse Press LLC. She is a highly revered, widely published poet and writer. She is the editor of numerous anthologies and serves as an editor of the Fine Lines Journal. Tomey-Zonneveld is the Poet Laureate of the Garden of Neuro Institute who champions emerging and established writers. Tomey-Zonneveld resides in Raleigh, North Carolina.

Cover design and graphics:
Kelli R. Jackson, a creative force to be reckoned with. Her creative genius at KRynae Design Co is expansive and unstoppable. Her designs include a growing collection of poetic images and promotions, personalized jackets, t-shirts and memorabilia for nonprofit organizations, and website design. A full-time mother of three, Kelli ensures that her children receive the creative nurturing that she craved as a child. Prior to the pandemic, Kelli Jackson served as Office Manager and Accounting Technician at the University of Colorado.

Foreword:

Chyrel J. Jackson, literary visionary and Amazon #1 Best Selling Author. She was reared and raised in the South Suburbs outside Chicago, Illinois, USA. The year 2021 garnered Chyrel her very first literary nomination: Pushcart Prize Nominee-Poem, "Love Unspoken," published in *Heart Beats Anthology.* In 2022 Chyrel was a contributing writer in the #1 Best Seller ranked Anthology, *Not Just Anybody Can Be Dad.* Jackson's personal publications, with her sister Lyris D. Wallace, are *Mirrored Images* and *Different Sides of the Same Coin.* This edgy writing duo appears in multiple published poetry anthologies and literary journals. You will find Chyrel J. Jackson always writing, creating written legacies one book at a time. Website: Sistersrocnrhyme.com

Back Cover Blurb:

Sarfraz Ahmed, romantic poet on a mission to spread love. He lives and works in East Midlands, United Kingdom. He has been writing poetry nearly twenty years and has contributed to many anthologies. His books include *Eighty-Four Pins* (June 2020), *My Teachers an Alien!* (November 2020 children's book with illustrator Natasha Adams), *Two Hearts* (February 2021 with Annette Tarpley), *Stab the Pomegranate* (2021), *The Gift of Poetry* (2022), and *Ramblings of a Romantic Poet* (2023). Ahmed is an administrator for the Passion of Poetry, a Facebook platform for emerging and esteemed poets. In May 2021, Ahmed was recognized by Poetry and Literature World Vision as a World Contributor Poet for his numerous literary contributions. Ahmed is active at open mic events and has shared his poetry globally.

Encore

You must be prepared to work always without applause.
~Ernest Hemingway

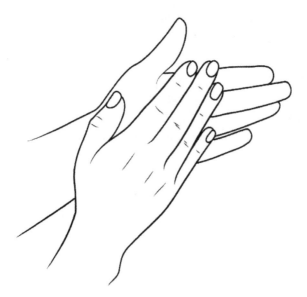

Printed in the USA
CPSIA information can be obtained
at www.ICGtesting.com
CBHW031835270923
1160CB00001B/8